Guess What!

Student's Book 1B

Susannah Reed with Kay Bentley
Series Editor: Lesley Koustaff

CAMBRIDGE
UNIVERSITY PRESS

Contents

5 My body

Guess What!

1 CD2 38 Listen. Who's speaking?

2 CD2 39 Listen, point, and say.

1 head

2 nose

3 eyes

BIKE CLUB

4 hair

5 ears

6 arms

7 mouth

8 hands

9 feet

10 legs

3 CD2 40 Listen and find.

Find Leo

4 CD2 41 **Say the chant.**

5 Think **Look and say the action.**

Number 1. Stamp your feet.

1

2

3

6 CD2 43 **Listen, look, and say.**

7 CD2 44 Think **Listen and say the name.**

i-Lin   i-Tex   i-Zak   i-Con

8 CD2 46 Sing the song.

9 Ask and answer.

Do you have a blue nose and two purple arms?

Number 3!

Yes, I do.

Grammar: *Do you have a yellow nose?* **63**

Value: Be clean

→ Workbook page 52

11   **Listen and act.**

Animal sounds

12 CD2 50 **Listen and say.**

An iguana
with pink ink.

What **sense** is it?

1 CD2 52 **Listen and say.**

 1
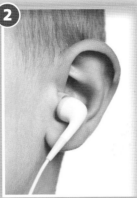 2
 3
 4
 5

sight　　　　hearing　　　　smell　　　　taste　　　　touch

2 **Watch the video.**

3 **Look and say the senses.**

Number 1. Sight and touch.　　Yes.

Guess What!

 1
 2

 3
 4

Project

4 **Make a senses poster.**

6 Food

Guess
What!

1 (CD3 02) **Listen. Who's speaking?**

2 (CD3 03) **Listen, point, and say.**

1 chicken
2 water
3 orange
4 cheese
5 milk
6 egg
7 apple
8 banana
9 juice
10 bread

3 (CD3 04) **Listen and find.**

Find Leo

4 CD3 05 **Say the chant.**

5 (Think) **Look and find five differences.**

Picture 1. I have chicken.

Picture 2. I have cheese.

6 CD3 07 **Listen, look, and say.**

7 CD3 08 (Think) **Listen and say the name.**

I like chicken, and I like bananas …   Kim.

		🍗	🍌	🥛	🧃
Alex		✗	✓	✗	✓
Sasha		✓	✗	✓	✗
Sam		✗	✓	✓	✗
Kim		✓	✓	✓	✗

8 CD3 10 Sing the song.

9 About Me Play the game.

Number 1. Yellow. Do you like chicken with apples?   No, I don't.

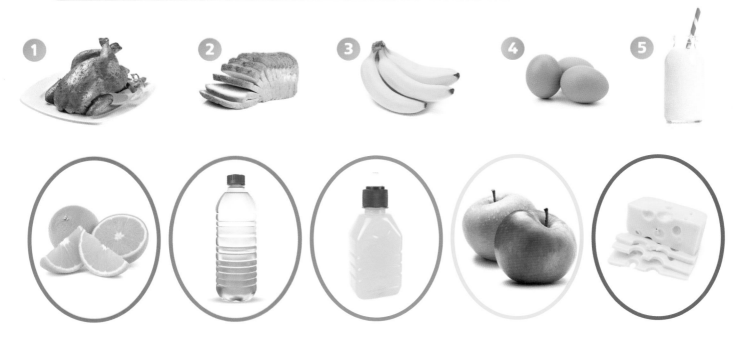

Grammar: *Do you like eggs?*

74 Value: Be patient

→ Workbook page 60

11 **CD3 13** **Talk Time** Listen and act.

Animal sounds

  12 **CD3 14** Listen and say.

An elephant with ten eggs.

Where is **food** from?

1 Listen and say.

plants

animals

2 Watch the video.

3 Look and say *plant* or *animal*.

Number 1. Plant. Yes!

Guess What!

Project

4 Make a food and drink poster.

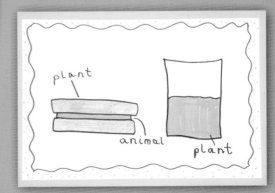

plant

animal   plant

Review **Units 5 and 6**

1 **Look and say the word.** Number 1. Mouth.

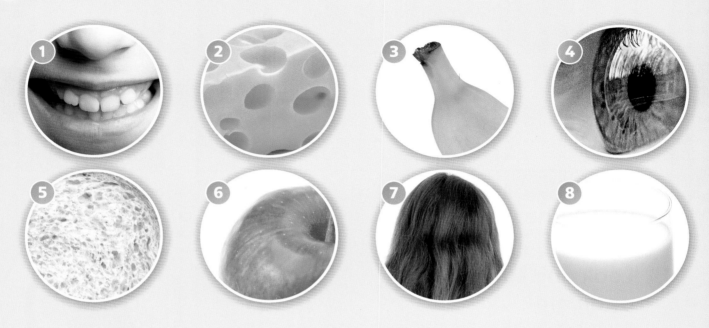

2 CD3 17 **Listen and say the name.**

Tony

Ana

Lily

Ravi

→ Workbook pages 64–65

3 Play the game.

Finish

Start

Blue
I don't have (four hands).
I have a (nose).

Green
I like / I don't like
(bananas).

79

(7) Actions

Guess! What!

1 (CD3 18) Listen. Who's speaking?

2 (CD3 19) Listen, point, and say.

Come to a **Festival** at the park!

1 run
2 jump
3 swim
4 climb
5 play soccer
6 ride a bike
7 draw
8 paint
9 dance
10 sing

3 (CD3 20) Listen and find.

Find Leo

4 CD3 21 Say the chant.

5 Look and match. Then say the action.

> Number 1. Green.
> Play soccer.

1
2
3
4

Vocabulary **83**

6 (CD3 23) **Listen, look, and say.**

①

②

7 (CD3 24) **Listen and say the number.** I can run. Six.

①

②

③

④

⑤

⑥

8 (CD3 26) **Sing the song.**

9   **Ask and answer.**

Can you ride a bike?

Yes, I can.

1

2

3

4

5

6

Value: Help your friends

→ Workbook page 70

11   **Listen and act.**

Animal sounds

12 CD3 30 **Listen and say.**

An **u**mbrella

bird can j**u**mp.

What's the
number?

1 CD3 32 Listen and say.

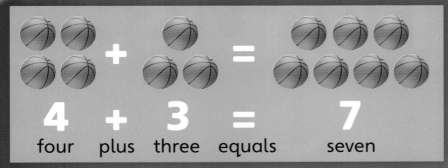

4 + 3 = 7

four plus three equals seven

8 – 2 = 6

eight minus two equals six

Guess What!

2 Watch the video.

3 Find the number. Then say the words.

Five balls plus five balls equals ten balls.   Yes!

(1)

(2)
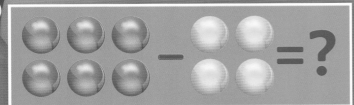

(3)
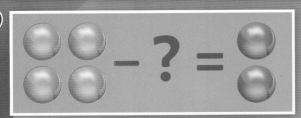

Project

4 Draw two picture sums.

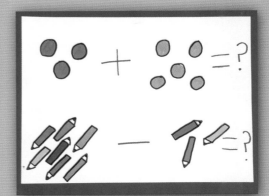

8 Animals

Guess What!

1 (CD3 33) Listen. Who's speaking?

2 (CD3 34) Listen, point, and say.

1 giraffe

2 monkey

3 elephant

4 bird

5 snake

6 hippo

7 zebra

Africa

8 lion

9 spider

10 crocodile

Find Leo

3 (CD3 35) Listen and find.

Say the chant.

 Think **Look and say the animal.**

Number 1. A snake.

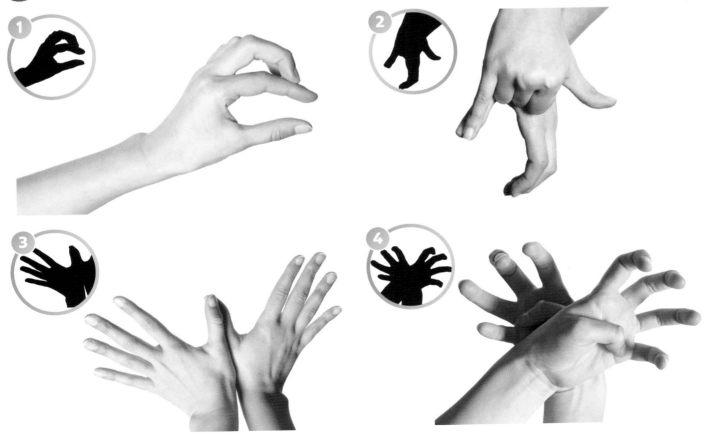

6 CD3 38 Listen, point, and say.

long   short

tall   short

big   small

7 CD3 39 Listen and say the number.

1

2

3

8 (CD3 40) **Sing the song.**

9 (CD3 41) **Listen and say *yes* or *no*.**

10 **Look and find five mistakes.**

Giraffes don't have short necks.
Giraffes have long necks.

Grammar: *Elephants have long trunks.* **95**

Value: Respect animals

→ Workbook page 78

12   **Listen and act.**

Animal sounds

13 **Listen and say.**

An **o**ctopus in an **o**range box.

How do animals move?

1 CD3 47 **Listen and say.**

walk

fly

slither

2 **Watch the video.**

3 **Look and say *walk*, *fly*, or *slither*.**

A spider can walk. Yes.

Guess What!

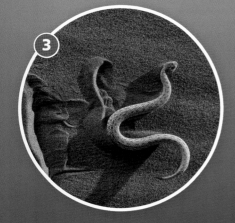

Project

4 **Make an animal movement chart.**

walk fly slither

Review Units 7 and 8

1 Look and say the words.

Number 1. Play soccer.

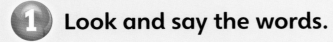

2 CD3 48 Listen and say the number.

→ Workbook pages 82–83

Play the game.

Orange
I can (play soccer).

Green
(Giraffes) have (long necks).

Red
(Birds) are (small).

My sounds

iguana

elephant

umbrella bird

octopus

Workbook 1B
with Online Resources

Contents

Susan Rivers

Series Editor: Lesley Koustaff

1 Read and circle the correct word.

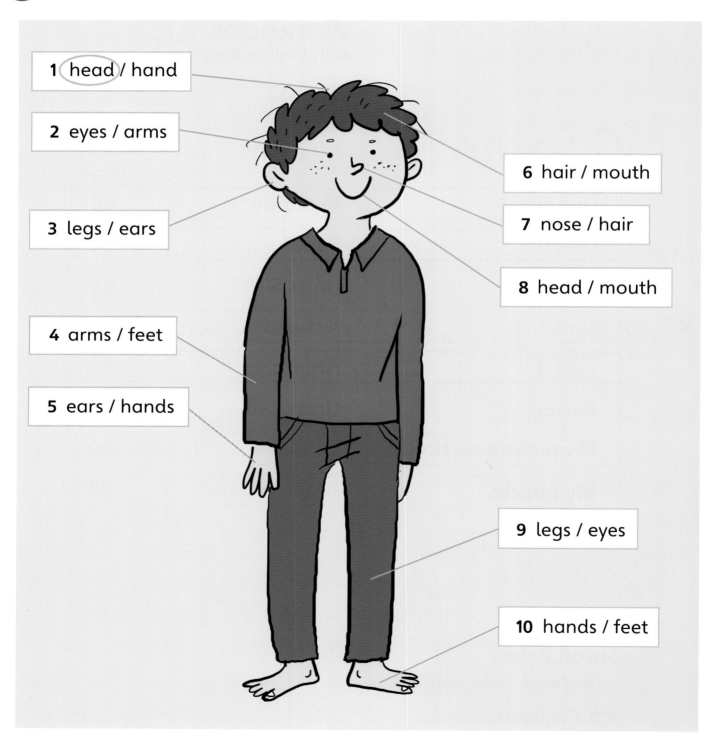

1 (head) / hand

2 eyes / arms

3 legs / ears

4 arms / feet

5 ears / hands

6 hair / mouth

7 nose / hair

8 head / mouth

9 legs / eyes

10 hands / feet

 **Listen and stick.**

3 **Look at the picture. Find and circle the words.**

h	e	a	d	e	p	n
l	e	g	l	a	l	o
h	h	k	o	r	j	s
a	a	e	r	t	y	e
i	r	w	h	a	n	d
r	m	o	u	t	h	n
q	n	v	f	e	e	t

 My picture dictionary → Go to page 84: Check the words you know and trace.

Vocabulary **49**

4 CD2 45 Listen and check ✓.

1	2	3
a	a	a
b ✓	b	b
c	c	c

5 Think What's different? Circle the word.

(eyes) / ears

feet / hands

legs / arms

mouth / nose

6 Look, read, and check ✓.

1

Do you have hair?

☐ Yes, I do.   ✓ No, I don't.

2

Do you have two arms?

☐ Yes, I do.   ☐ No, I don't.

3

Do you have four legs?

☐ Yes, I do.   ☐ No, I don't.

4

Do you have one nose?

☐ Yes, I do.   ☐ No, I don't.

7 Draw a robot. Then complete the sentences.

I have _____

_____ .

I don't have _____

_____ .

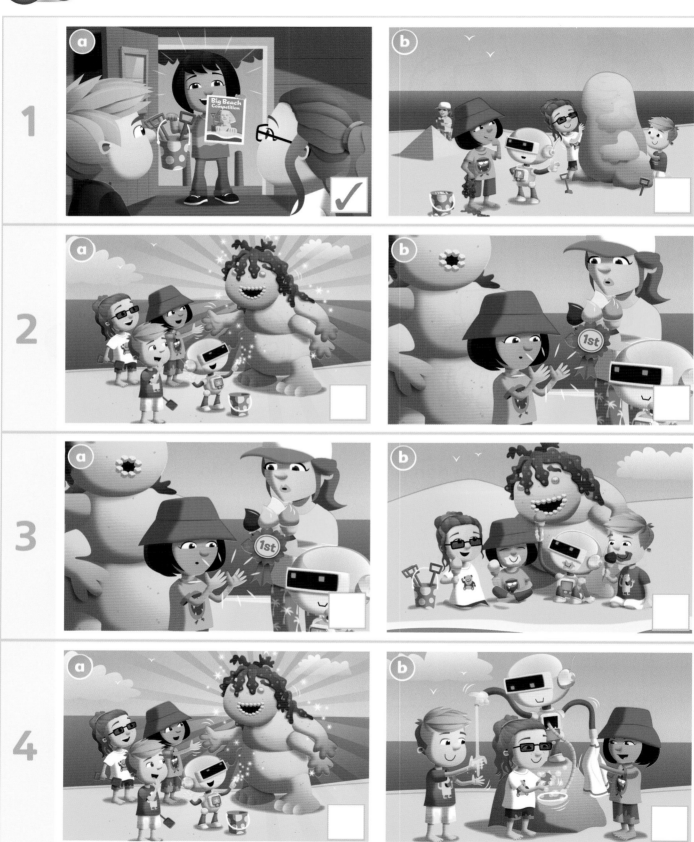

9 **What's missing? Look and draw. Then stick.**

I'm clean.

10 **Trace the letters.**

An iguana
with pink ink.

11 (CD2 51) **Listen and circle the *i* words.**

1
2
3
4

What sense is it?

1 Look, read, and match.

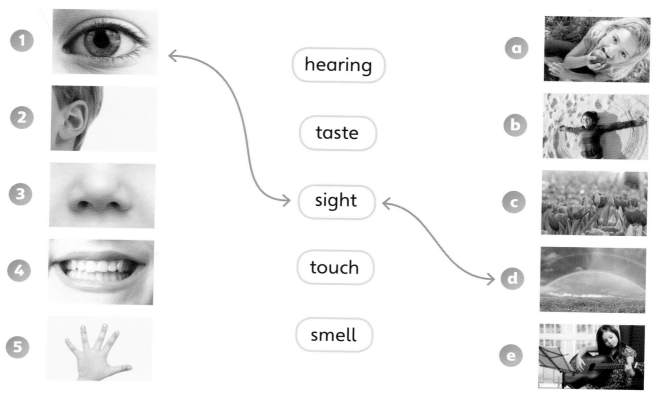

1   hearing   a
2   taste   b
3   sight   c
4   touch   d
5   smell   e

2 Look and check ✓.

	👁	👂	👃	😁	🖐
	✓				

Evaluation

1 **Look, match, and trace. Then read and say.**

1 2 3 4

head   feet

ears   nose

2 What's your favorite part? Use your stickers.

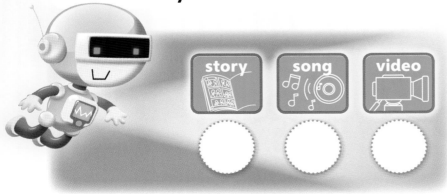

story   song   video

3  **Complete the color.**

b_u_

Then go to page 88 and color the Unit 5 pieces.

6 Food

1 Look and write the word.

1

k m l i
milk

2

p e a l p
_____

3

g e g
_____

4
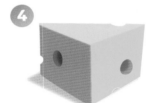
c e h s e e
_____

5

a e w r t
_____

6

a a a n n b
_____

2 Complete the words and match.

1 jui c e   **2** o _ a n g e   **3** b _ e a d   **4** c _ i c k _ n

a    **b**    **c**    **d**

3 CD3 06  **Listen and stick.**

① ②

③ ④

4 Think **Look and write the words.**

~~cheese~~   an apple   juice   bread   water
a banana   an egg   an orange   chicken   milk

We eat …
1 _cheese_
2 _____
3 _____
4 _____
5 _____
6 _____
7 _____

We drink …
1 _____
2 _____
3 _____

My picture dictionary → Go to page 85: Check the words you know and trace.

5 CD3 09 **Listen and check ✓ or put an ✗.**

1			✓	✗
2				
3				
4				

6 **Look, read, and circle.**

1  I **like** / (**don't like**) juice.

2  I **like** / **don't like** oranges.

3  I **like** / **don't like** bread.

4  I **like** / **don't like** water.

5  I **like** / **don't like** apples.

6  I **like** / **don't like** eggs.

7 Look, read, and check ✓.

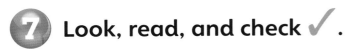

1

Do you like bread?

✓ Yes, I do. ☐ No, I don't.

2

Do you like eggs?

☐ Yes, I do. ☐ No, I don't.

3

Do you like bananas?

☐ Yes, I do. ☐ No, I don't.

4

Do you like juice?

☐ Yes, I do. ☐ No, I don't.

8 (About Me) Look and answer the questions with *Yes, I do* or *No, I don't.*

1 Do you like chicken?

_____.

2 Do you like milk?

_____.

3 Do you like cheese?

_____.

4 Do you like bananas?

_____.

CD3 12 **Listen, look, and match.**

10 **What's missing? Look and draw. Then stick.**

I'm patient.

a

b

c

11 **Trace the letters.**

An elephant with ten eggs.

12 CD3 15 **Listen and circle the e words.**

1

2

3

4

Where is food from?

1 Look and check ✓ or put an ✗.

Plants

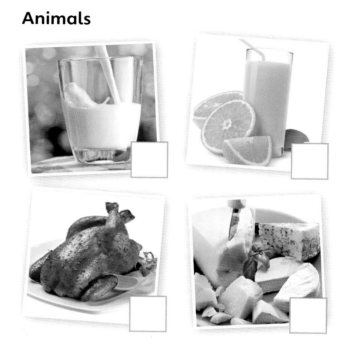

✓

Animals

2 Look, read, and circle.

1
(plant)/ animal

2
plant / animal

3
plant / animal

4
plant / animal

5
plant / animal

6
plant / animal

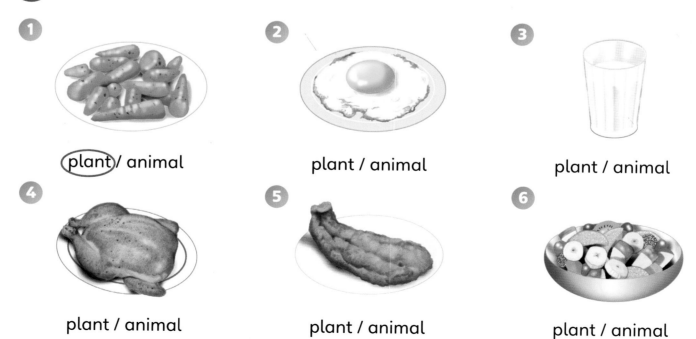

Evaluation

1 **Look, match, and write. Then read and say.**

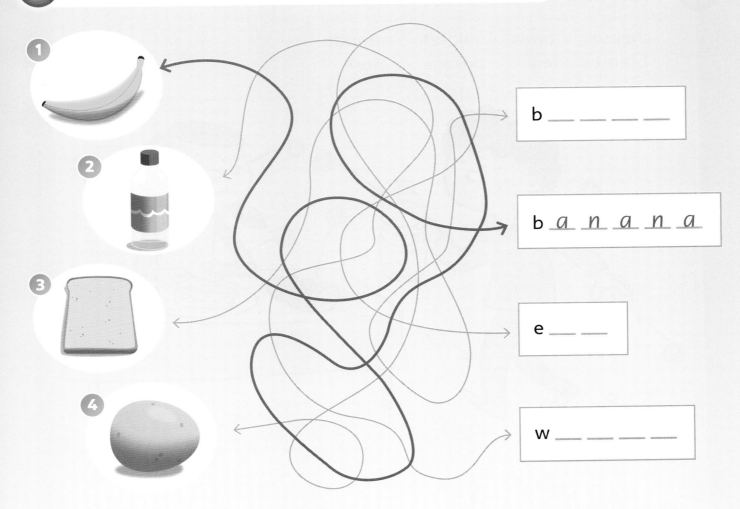

1

2

3

4

b _ _ _ _ _

b a n a n a

e _ _ _

w _ _ _ _ _ _

2 **What's your favorite part? Use your stickers.**

story   song   video

3 **Puzzle** **Write the color.**

p e u l r p _ _ _ _ _

Then go to page 88 and color the Unit 6 pieces.

Review Units 5 and 6

1 Look and write.

cheese   ~~arms~~   water   mouth
bread   legs   orange   nose

1 _arms_   2 _____

3 _____   4 _____

5 _____   6 _____

7 _____   8 _____

2 Read and match.

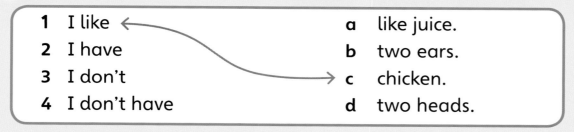

1 I like   a   like juice.
2 I have   b   two ears.
3 I don't   c   chicken.
4 I don't have   d   two heads.

Write the question. Then check ✓ .

1

you / three / Do / have / hands / ?

Do you have three hands?

☐ Yes, I do. ✓ No, I don't.

2

like / eggs / you / Do / ?

_____

☐ Yes, I do. ☐ No, I don't.

3

have / two / you / Do / ears / ?

_____

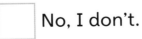

☐ Yes, I do. ☐ No, I don't.

4

you / Do / milk / like / ?

_____

☐ Yes, I do. ☐ No, I don't.

1 Look, read, and circle the word.

swim / (sing)

climb / paint

dance / draw

ride a bike / play soccer

2 Look at the pictures. Find and circle the words.

runswimjumppaintclimb(dance)

3 CD3 22 Listen and stick.

4 Think Read and circle the object.

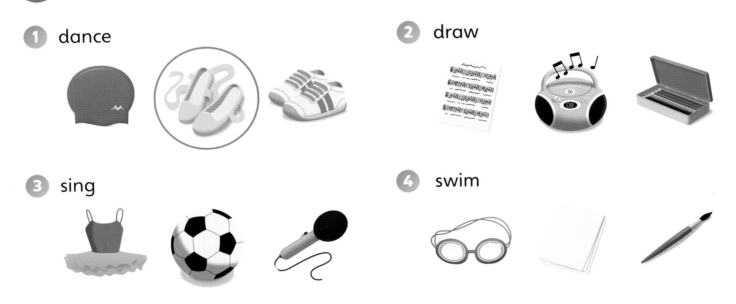

1 dance

2 draw

3 sing

4 swim

My picture dictionary → Go to page 86: Check the words you know and trace.

Vocabulary **67**

5 CD3 25 **Listen and circle the picture.**

1

2

3

4

6 **Look and write *can* or *can't*.**

1 I ___can___ run.   **2** I _____ draw.

3 I _____ climb.   **4** I _____ dance.

7 **Look, read, and check ✓ .**

1

Can you swim?

☐ Yes, I can.   ✓ No, I can't.

2

Can you jump?

☐ Yes, I can.   ☐ No, I can't.

3

Can you ride a bike?

☐ Yes, I can.   ☐ No, I can't.

4

Can you dance?

☐ Yes, I can.   ☐ No, I can't.

8 (About Me) **Complete the chart. Ask three friends and check ✓ .**

Name			
1 _Me_			
2			
3			
4			

Can you sing?   Yes, I can. / No, I can't.

9 Listen and number.

1

10 **What's missing? Look and draw. Then stick.**

I help my friends.

11 **Trace the letters.**

An umbrella
bird can jump.

12 CD3 31 **Listen and circle the *u* words.**

1  2  3  4

What's the number?

1 Think and write the answer. Then color.

1 1 + 1 = [2] red   **2** 2 + 4 = [ ] blue

3 3 + 6 = [ ] orange   **4** 10 − 2 = [ ] purple

5 5 − 2 = [ ] green   **6** 8 − 4 = [ ] yellow

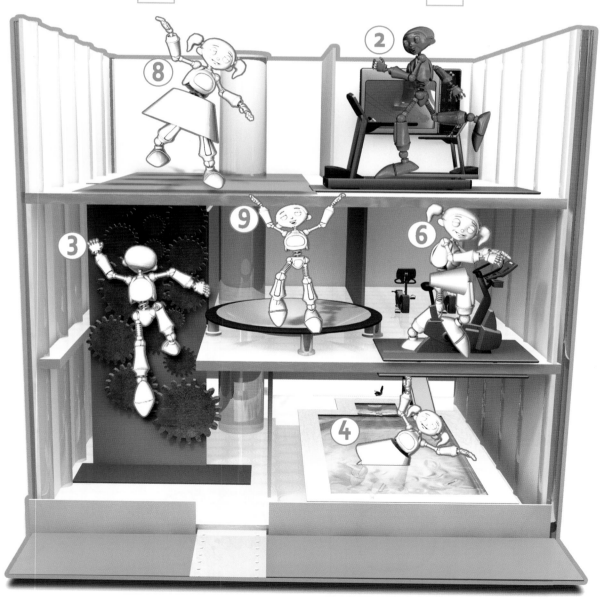

Evaluation

1 Look and write the words. Then read and say.

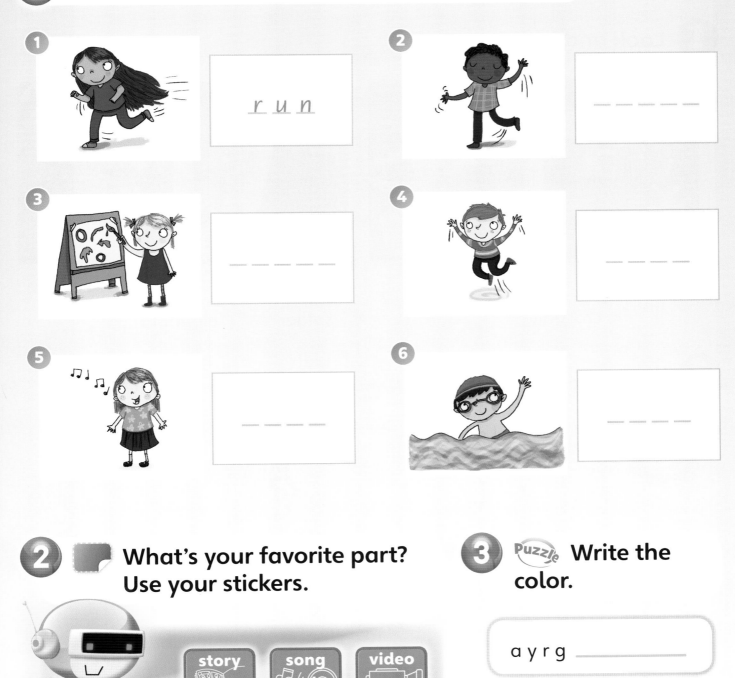

1 r u n

2 ___ ___ ___ ___

3 ___ ___ ___ ___ ___

4 ___ ___ ___

5 ___ ___ ___ ___

6 ___ ___ ___ ___

2 What's your favorite part? Use your stickers.

story   song   video

3 Puzzle Write the color.

a y r g _____

Then go to page 88 and color the Unit 7 pieces.

8 Animals

1 Look and match.

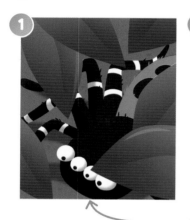
1

2

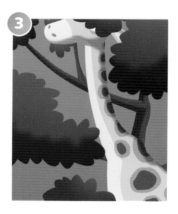
3

4

a crocodile   **b** giraffe   **c** spider   **d** elephant

2 Look and write the word.

1

n l o i

lion

2

b e r z a

_____

3

i d b r

_____

4

o i p h p

_____

5

m y o e k n

_____

6

e a k n s

_____

3 CD3 37 Listen and stick.

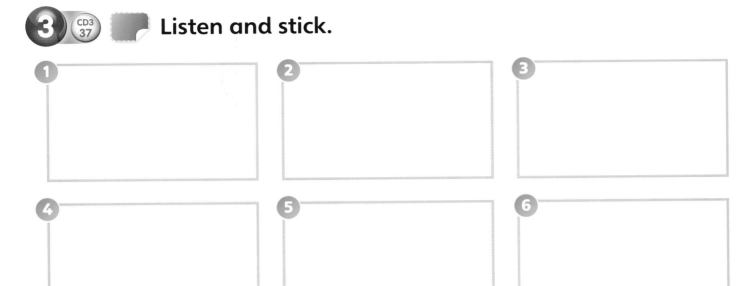

| 1 | 2 | 3 |
| 4 | 5 | 6 |

4 Think Write the words. Circle the animals with four legs.

snake   spider   bird   ~~zebra~~   elephant   giraffe   hippo   lion

1 zebra

2

3

4

5

6

7

8

My picture dictionary → Go to page 87: Check the words you know and trace.

5 Look and match the opposites.

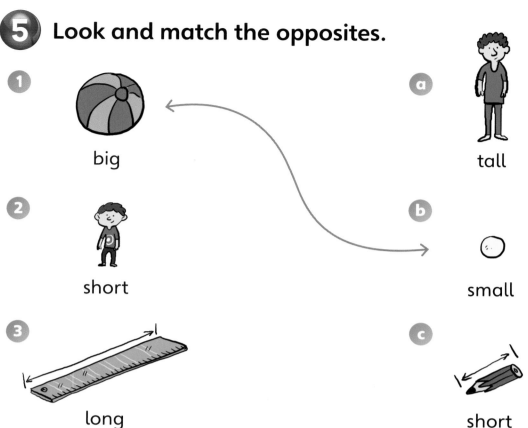

1 big

2 short

3 long

a tall

b small

c short

6 Look, read, and complete the sentences.

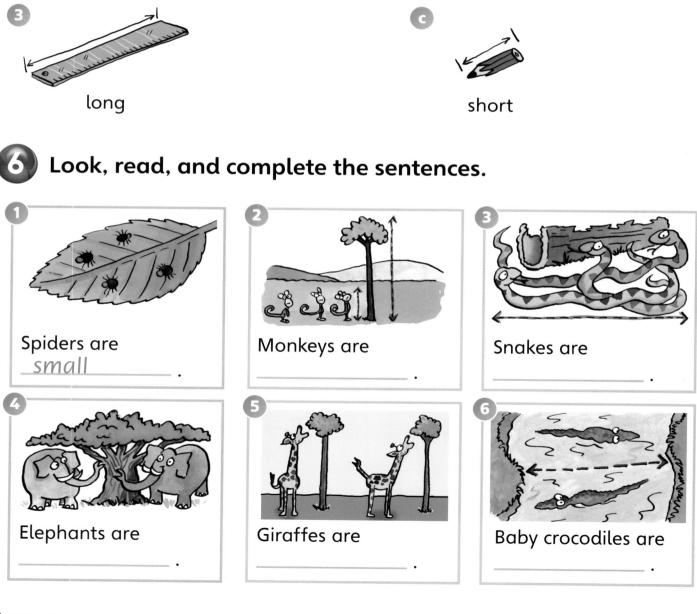

1 Spiders are
small .

2 Monkeys are
_____ .

3 Snakes are
_____ .

4 Elephants are
_____ .

5 Giraffes are
_____ .

6 Baby crocodiles are
_____ .

7 **Look and read. Circle the correct sentences.**

1

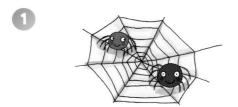

Spiders have wings.

2

Elephants have long trunks.

3

Hippos have long necks.

4

Monkeys have long tails.

8 **Look and write.**

big teeth   long tails   ~~small wings~~   long necks   short legs

1 Birds have _small_ _wings_ .

2 Zebras have _____ _____ .

3 Hippos have _____ _____ .

4 Giraffes have _____ _____ .

5 Birds have _____ _____ .

9 (About Me) **Ask and answer with a friend.**

What are your favorite animals?   Elephants.

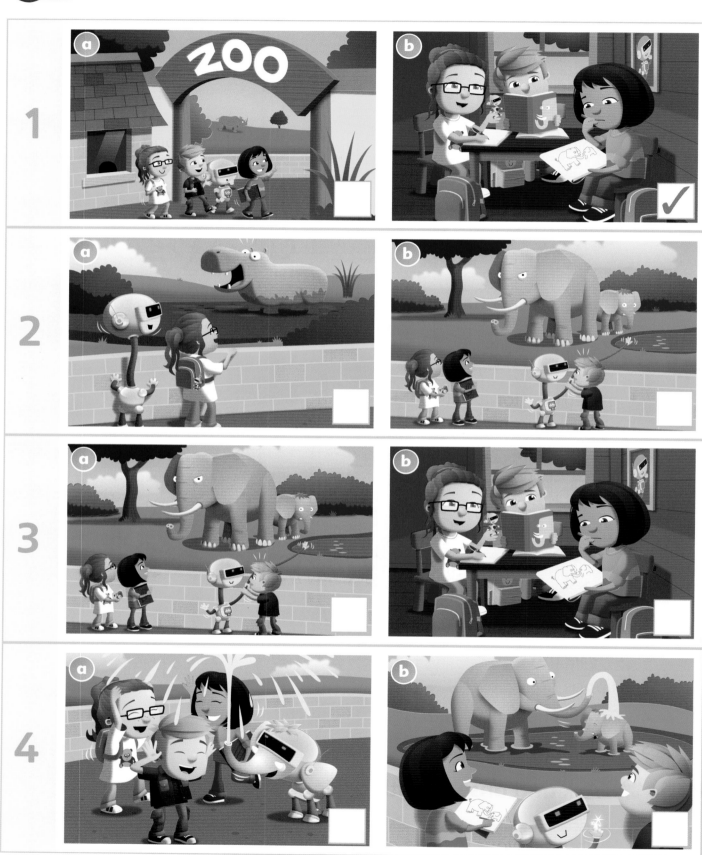

11 What's missing? Look and draw. Then stick.

I respect animals.

12 Trace the letters.

An octopus in an orange box.

13 CD3 46 Listen and circle the *o* words.

1   2   3   4

How do **animals** move?

1 **Read and complete. Then number the pictures.**

slither	~~walk~~	fly	walk

1 An elephant can ___walk___ .   **2** A snake can _____ .

3 A bird can _____ .   **4** A giraffe can _____ .

a

b

c

d

1

2 **Look at Activity 1 and circle the answers.**

1 Can a snake fly?   Yes, it can. / No, it can't.

2 Can an elephant walk?   Yes, it can. / No, it can't.

3 Can a bird fly?   Yes, it can. / No, it can't.

4 Can a giraffe slither?   Yes, it can. / No, it can't.

Evaluation

1 **Look and write the word. Then read and say.**

1. z e b r a
2. _ _ _ _ _
3. _ _ _ _ _
4. _ _ _ _ _ _ _ _
5. _ _ _ _ _ _ _
6. _ _ _ _ _

2 What's your favorite part? Use your stickers.

story   song   video

3 Puzzle **Write the color.**

l c k a b _____

Then go to page 88 and color the Unit 8 pieces.

Review Units 7 and 8

1 Look and write. Then draw number 9.

1 

2 

3 

4 

					9								
1				z	e	b	r	a					
2						a			o		c		r
3	s		a										
4		j											
5						i		p					
6						n		e					
7				o			e						
8		a		n									

5 

6 

7 

8 

9

2 Look and write.

soccer   small   long necks   a bike   ~~swim~~

1 Can you ___swim___ ?
2 Birds are _____ .
3 I can play _____ .
4 Giraffes have _____ .
5 I can't ride _____ .

3 Look, read, and circle the words.

1  (Snakes) / **Spiders** are long.

2  I **can** / **can't** sing.

3  Hippos **have** / **don't have** short tails.

4  I can **draw** / **dance**.

5 My body

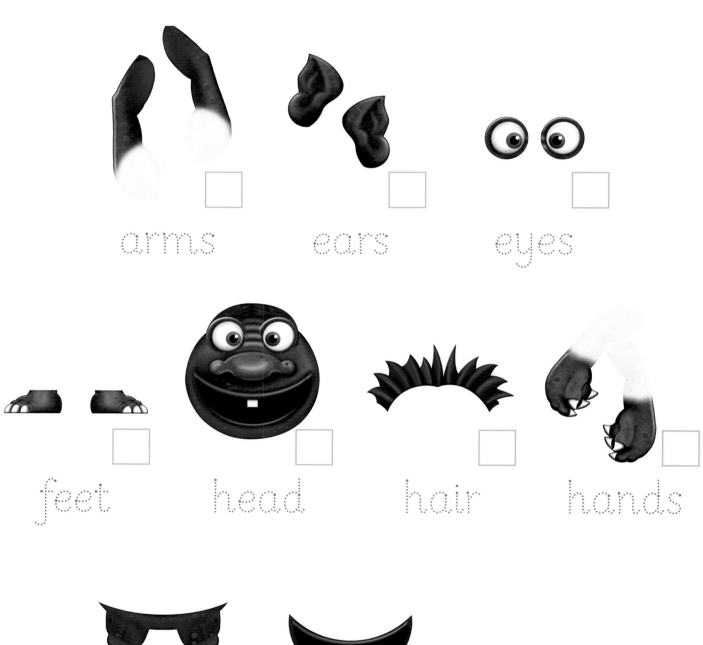

arms ☐ ears ☐ eyes ☐

feet ☐ head ☐ hair ☐ hands ☐

legs ☐ mouth ☐ nose ☐

6 Food

apple   banana   bread

cheese   chicken   egg   juice

milk   orange   water

7 Actions

climb

dance

draw

jump

paint

play soccer

ride a bike

run

sing

swim

8 Animals

bird

crocodile

elephant

giraffe

hippo

lion

monkey

snake

spider

zebra

My puzzle

Thanks and Acknowledgements

Many thanks to everyone in the excellent team at Cambridge University Press. In particular we would like to thank Emily Hird, Liane Grainger, Camilla Agnew, and Flavia Lamborghini whose professionalism, enthusiasm, experience, and talent makes them all such a pleasure to work with.

We would also like to give special thanks to Lesley Koustaff for her unfailing support, expert guidance, good humor, and welcome encouragement throughout the project.

The authors and publishers would like to thank the following contributors:
Blooberry Design: concept design, cover design, book design, page makeup
Emma Szlachta, Vicky Bewick: editing
Lisa Hutchins: freelance editing
Ann Thomson: art direction, picture research
Gareth Boden: commissioned photography
Jon Barlow: commissioned photography
Ian Harker: audio recording
Robert Lee, Dib Dib Dub Studios: song and chant composition
Vince Cross: theme tune composition
James Richardson: arrangement of theme tune
John Marshall Media: audio recording and production
Phaebus: video production
hyphen S.A.: publishing management, American English edition

The authors and publishers acknowledge the following sources of copyright material and are grateful for the permissions granted. Although every effort has been made, it has not always been possible to identify the sources of all the material used, or to trace all copyright holders.

If any omissions are brought to our notice, we will be happy to include the appropriate acknowledgments on reprinting.

The authors and publishers would like to thank the following illustrators:

Student's Book
Chris Jevons (Bright Agency): pp 62, 84, 95; Joelle Dreidemy (Bright Agency): pp 61, 71; Kirsten Collier (Bright Agency): pp 65, 75, 87, 97, 102; Marcus Cutler (Sylvie Poggio): pp 79, 101; Marek Jagucki: pp 59, 60, 64, 69, 70, 74, 81, 82, 86, 91, 92, 96; Richard Watson (Bright Agency): pp 84; Woody Fox (Bright Agency): pp 63, 73, 85, 95

Workbook
Marek Jagucki p52, 55, 56, 60, 63, 67, 70, 73, 74, 78, 79, 81, 88, stickers; Joelle Dreidemy (Bright Agency) p48, 49, 51, 55, 57, 59, 64, 66, 69, 76, 83; Woody Fox (Bright Agency) p50, 53, 58, 61, 65, 66, 68, 69, 71, 75, 76, 77, 81, 82, stickers; Sarah Jennings (Bright Agency) p50, 53, 56, 58, 61, 68, 71, 73, 74, 77, 79, stickers; Mark Duffin p72; Graham Kennedy p62; Hardinge (Monkey Feet) p84, 85, 86, 87

The authors and publishers would like to thank the following for permission to reproduce photographs:

Student's Book
p.65 (B/G), p.87 (B/G): SZE FEI WONG/Getty Images; p.97 (B/G): Jolanta Wojcicka/Shutterstock; p.75 (B/G): Tim Jackson/Getty Images; p.58–59: Frans Lemmens/ Corbis; p.61 (TL): Pavel L Photo and Video/Shutterstock; p.61 (TC girl): Gelpi JM/Shutterstock; p.61 (TC boy): Tetra Images/Alamy; p.61 (TR): annie-claude/ Getty Images; p.66–67: gettyimages/Maria Pavlova; p.67 (T-1): Shutterstock/ Federico Rostagno; p.67 (T-2): Shutterstock/ Ilya Andriyanov; p.67 (T-3): Evgeny Bakharev/Shutterstock; p.67 (T-4): acilo/ Getty Images; p.67 (T-5): YAY Media AS/ Alamy; p.67 (B-1): Valentia_G/Shutterstock; p.67 (B-2): sbarabu/Shutterstock; p.67 (B-3): foodfolio/Alamy; p.67 (B-4): Liunian/shutterstock; p.68–69: Christian Mueller/Shutterstock; p.71 (TL): Serg Salivon/Shutterstock; p.71 (TR): Sea Wave/ Shutterstock; p.71 (CL): ThomsonD/Shutterstock; p.71 (CR): Chursina Viktorlia/ Shutterstock; p.72 (CL), p.73 (1): Viktor1/Shutterstock; P.72 (C bananas): Sergio33/Shutterstock; p.72 (C milk): Tarasyuk Igor/Shutterstock; p.72 (CR): Anna Kucherova/Shutterstock; p.72 (Alex): R. Gino Santa Maria/ Shutterstock; p.72 (Sasha): Jack Hollingsworth/Getty Images; p.72 (Sam): KidStock/Getty Images; p.72 (Kim): Wavebreakmedia Ltd/Getty Images; p.73 (2): v.s.anandhakrishna/ Shutterstock; p.73 (3): saiko3p/Getty Images; p.73 (4), p.73 (BL): Nattika/ Shutterstock; p.73 (5): Christopher Elwell/ Shutterstock; p.73 (water): Betacam- SP/Shutterstock; p.73 (juice): Kitch Bain/Shutterstock; p.73 (apples): Garsya/ Shutterstock; p.73 (BR): aarrows/ Shutterstock; p.76–77: R. Fassbind/Shutterstock; p.77 (T-1): Shutterstock/ colognephotos; p.77 (T-2): Shutterstock/Denis and Yulia Pogostins; p.77 (T-3): pattyphotoart/Shutterstock; p.77 (T-4): Shutterstock/ lightpoet; p.77 (T-5): Shutterstock/holbox; p.77 (T-6): Zoe mack/Alamy; p.77 (B-1): Julian Rovagnati/Shutterstock; p.77 (B-2): Anna Moskvina/Shutterstock; p.77 (B-3): Shutterstock/ffolas; p.77 (B-4): PeJo/Shutterstock; p.78 (1): Shutterstock/xavier gallego morel; p.78 (2): Shutterstock/Christian Draghici; p.78 (3): Shutterstock/ Svetlana Kuznetsova; p.78 (4): Shutterstock/janinajaak; p.78 (5): Shutterstock/ andersphoto; p.78 (6): ell2550/Shutterstock; p.78 (7): Shutterstock/VaclavHroch; p.78 (8): Shutterstock/Valentyn Volkov; p.80–81: Juniors Bildarchiv BmbH/Alamy; p.83 (1): Shutterstock/irin-k; p.83 (2): Shutterstock/Picsfive; p.83 (3): Shutterstock/ Luminis; p.83 (4): Shutterstock/ auremar; p.83 (BL): Shutterstock/Pressmaster; p.83 (BC swim), p.83 (BR): Shutterstock/Monkey Business Images; p.83 (BC paint): Shutterstock/Len44ik; p.88–89: Jose Luis Stephens/Getty Images; p.89 (T): Shutterstock/R-O-M-A; p.89 (C): Shutterstock/silavsale; p.90–91: Villiers Steyn/Shutterstock; p.93 (TL): Stuart Westmorland/Getty Images; p.93 (TC monkey): Don Mammoser/Shutterstock; p.93 (TC bird): Danita Delimont/Getty Images; p.93 (TR): A.Tofke Cologne Germay/Getty Images; p.94 (TL): Maurizio Biso/ Shutterstock; p.94 (TR): Matt Ragen/Shutterstock; p.94 (CL): Volodymyr Burdiak/Shutterstock; p.94 (BL): Lintao Zhang/Getty Images; p.94 (BC): Heiko Kiera/Shutterstock; p.94 (BR): PILAR OLIVARES/Reuters/Corbis; p.97 (T): Erica Shires/Corbis; p.98–99: Joe McDonald/Corbis; p.99 (TL): john michael evan potter/Shutterstock; p.99 (TC): Istvan Kadar Photography/Getty Images; p.99 (TR): Purcell Pictures, Inc./Alamy; p.99 (CL): Petra Wegner/ Alamy; p.99 (C): Mmphotos/Getty Images; p.99 (BL): Solvin Zankl/Nature Picture Library/Corbis; p.99 (BC): Juniors Bildarchiv BmbH/ Alamy; p.100 (T-1): Sally Anscombe/Getty Images; p.100 (T-2): DENIS-HUOT/ hemis.fr; p.100 (T-3): Ableimages/Getty Images; p.100 (T-4): Picture by Tambako the Jaguar/Getty Images; p.100 (T-5): David Muir/Getty Images; p.100 (T-6): Aldo Pavan/Getty Images; p.100 (T-7): GEN UMEKITA/Getty Images; p.100 (T-8): Larry Keller,Lititz Pa./Getty Images; p.100 (CL): Frank Krahmer/Getty Images; p.100 (CR): LeonP/Shutterstock; p.100 (BL): Dethan Punalur/Getty Images; p.100 (BR): Gallo Images – Heinrich van den Berg/Getty Images.

Commissioned photography by Gareth Boden: p.67 (BR), p.77 (BR), p.89 (BR), p.93 (B), p.99 (BR); Jon Barlow: p.63 (B), p.65 (T), p.72 (T), p.75 (T), p.78 (C), p.78 (B), p.83 (T), p.85 (B), p.87 (T)

Workbook
p. 48 (unit header): © Frans Lemmens/Corbis; p. 54 (header): Maria Pavlova/ Getty Images; p. 54 (Ex 1: photo 1) and p. 54 (Ex 2: eye): PhotoHouse/Shutterstock; p. 54 (Ex 1: photo 2) and p. 54 (Ex 2: ear): Shane White/Shutterstock; p. 54 (Ex 1: photo 3) and p. 54 (Ex 2: nose): RusN/Getty Images; p. 54 (Ex 1: photo 4) and p. 54 (Ex 2: mouth): Hemera Technologies/Getty Images; p. 54 (Ex 1: photo 5) and p. 54 (Ex 2: hand): kzww/Shutterstock; p. 54 (Ex 1: photo a): Monkey Business Images/Getty Images; p. 54 (Ex 1: photo b): Jessica Peterson/Getty Images; p. 54 (Ex 1: photo c): ostsaga/Getty Images; p. 54 (Ex 1: photo d): Pichugin Dmitry/Shutterstock; p. 54 (Ex 1: photo e): AntonioDiaz/Shutterstock; p. 54 (Ex 2: drawing): iropa/Getty Images; p. 54 (Ex 2: drum): Elena Schweitzer/Shutterstock; p. 54 (Ex 2: teddy bear): Agorohov/ Shutterstock; p. 54 (Ex 2: ice-cream): anskuw/Getty Images; p. 54 (Ex 2: sea): Digital Vision/Getty Images; p. 56 (unit header): Christian Mueller/Shutterstock; p. 62 (header): R. Fassbind/Shutterstock; p. 62 (banana): M. Unal Ozmen/Shutterstock; p. 62 (egg): NinaM/Shutterstock; p. 62 (tomatoes): Anna Kucherova/Shutterstock; p. 62 (orange): Natikka/Shutterstock; p. 62 (milk): Efired/Shutterstock; p. 62 (juice): Anna Kucherova/Shutterstock; p. 62 (chicken): Viktor1/Shutterstock; p. 62 (cheese): MaraZe/Shutterstock; p. 66 (unit header): © Juniors Bildarchiv GmbH/Alamy; p. 72 (header): Jose Luis Stephens/Getty Images; p. 74 (unit header): Villiers Steyn/Shutterstock; p. 80 (header): © Joe McDonald/Corbis; p. 80 (Ex 1: giraffe): Volanthevist/Getty Images; p. 80 (Ex 1: bird): Owen Price/Getty Images; p. 80 (Ex 1: snake): Kristian Bell/Getty Images; p. 80 (Ex 1: elephant): brodtcast/Getty Images.

Our special thanks to the following for their kind help during location photography:

Radmore Farm Shop, Queen Emma primary School

Front Cover photo by **Premium/UIG/Getty Images**

Front Cover illustration by **Premium/UIG/Getty Images**

 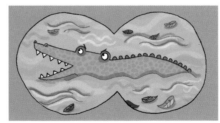 

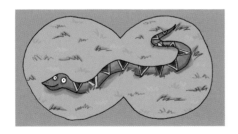